Corrupted into Song

Corrupted into Song

The Complete Poems of Alvin Feinman

Edited by Deborah Dorfman

*With a foreword by Harold Bloom
and an introduction by James Geary*

PRINCETON UNIVERSITY PRESS

PRINCETON AND OXFORD

Published by Princeton University Press, 41 William Street, Princeton, New Jersey 08540
In the United Kingdom: Princeton University Press, 6 Oxford Street, Woodstock, Oxfordshire OX20 1TW

press.princeton.edu

Jacket art: *The Written Sea* © Estate of John Marin / Artists Rights Society (ARS), New York

The present volume contains previously unpublished poems in addition to the complete text of *Poems*, published by Princeton University Press in 1990, which included poems first published in *Preambles and Other Poems,* Oxford University Press, 1964, with some revisions. A version of "The Tree" appeared in *Harper's Magazine*, copyright © 1970. Reprinted from the October issue by special permission.

Frontispiece photo of Alvin Feinman courtesy of Deborah Dorfman.

ISBN 978-0-691-17052-7

ISBN (pbk.) 978-0-691-17053-4

Library of Congress Control Number: 2015956951

British Library Cataloging-in-Publication Data is available

This book has been composed in Sabon LT Std

Printed on acid-free paper. ∞

Printed in the United States of America

10 9 8 7 6 5 4 3 2 1

Contents

Foreword

By Harold Bloom

I first met Alvin Feinman in September 1951, the day before I encountered another remarkable young man who also became a lifelong friend, Angus Fletcher. Alvin was twenty-two, a year older than we were, and a graduate student in philosophy at Yale, where Angus and I were students of literature. Alvin, to my lasting sorrow, died in 2008. Of my closest friends I am fortunate still to have Angus, having lost Alvin, Archie Ammons, and John Hollander, three superb poets and majestic intellects.

I am no poet; I cannot forget. Many of my friends are or were poets: Mark Strand, a recent loss; Robert Penn Warren, and happily still with us, William Merwin, John Ashbery, Jay Wright; and younger figures: Rosanna Warren, Henri Cole, Martha Serpas, Peter Cole.

Alvin at twenty-two was already a poet of astonishing individuation: the emergence of voice in him clarified as rapidly as it had in Rimbaud and Hart Crane. I recall reading the first of his three "Relic" poems sometime in October 1951:

> I will see her stand
> half a step back of the edge of some high place
> or at a leafless tree in some city park
> or seated with her knees toward me and her face turned
> > toward the window
>
> And always the tips of the fingers of both her hands
> will pull or twist at a handkerchief
> like lovely dead birds at a living thing
> trying to work apart something exquisitely, unreasonably
> > joined.

A month later I was introduced by Alvin to this beautiful, intense young woman in New York. Though lovers, she and my friend seemed remote from one another. I watched her hands in constant motion tugging at a handkerchief and wondered silently at the dispassionate tone of the eight-line lyric so precisely called "Relic."

Reciting the poem to myself these 60 years I have come to see its relationship to Eliot's farewell to Emily Hale:

La Figlia Che Piange

Stand on the highest pavement of the stair—
Lean on a garden urn—
Weave, weave the sunlight in your hair—
Clasp your flowers to you with a pained surprise—
Fling them to the ground and turn
With a fugitive resentment in your eyes:
But weave, weave the sunlight in your hair.

The dominant influences upon Feinman's poetry were Hart Crane, Wallace Stevens, T. S. Eliot, Paul Valéry, Rimbaud, Georg Trakl, and the earlier Rilke. I have listed them in the order of their importance in helping form his style and stance. Feinman's prime precursor was Hart Crane, and like the poet of *White Buildings* and *The Bridge,* my friend began with a volume of difficult yet frequently radiant lyrics. Unlike Crane, Feinman was not able to go on to the larger form of a visionary romance, and his inability to continue doomed his remarkable volume to neglect.

Returning to *Preambles and Other Poems* floods me with memories. I had taken the little book to my editor at the Oxford University Press, the late Whitney Blake, and urged him to publish it though not even a single poem had appeared in a magazine. Whitney discerned the high value of Alvin's poetry and agreed to publish it if I could provide endorsements by other poets and critics. Conrad Aiken, Allen Tate, R.W.B. Lewis, John Hollander, and Geoffrey Hartman joined me in support of the new poet. Hartman made a memorable comment:

> Thought thinks its ruin here without widening speculation. It finds what will not suffice. . . . Yet Feinman's poetry performs so total an *epoché* on "discursions fated and inept" that only the stumble toward a preamble is left. For so rigorous a sensibility, writing verse must be like crossing a threshold guarded by demons. . . .

The French critic Marcel Raymond characterized Paul Valéry's *La jeune parque* and "The Marine Cemetery" as a ceaseless agon between absolute consciousness and the acceptance of natural mutability:

> In them, a struggle takes place between two contrary attitudes: the pure (absolute) attitude, that of consciousness entrenching itself in its isolation, and the opposite, or impure attitude, that of the mind accepting life, change, action, giving up its dream of perfect integrity and allowing itself to be beguiled by things and captivated by their changing forms.

These two attitudes can be defined as total detachment or total involvement. In Valéry these contrary stances exist simultaneously. Feinman's total detachment purchases its freedom at the expense of a world of mutable splendors. The astonishing clarity of his best poems makes them expensive torsos rather than comprehensive visions.

Alvin Feinman's difficult fusion makes it a strenuous act of readership to decide where the visual and the purely visionary part in him:

November Sunday Morning

And the light, a wakened heyday of air
Tuned low and clear and wide,
A radiance now that would emblaze
And veil the most golden horn
Or any entering of a sudden clearing
To a standing, astonished, revealed . . .

That the actual streets I loitered in
Lay lit like fields, or narrow channels
About to open to a burning river;
All brick and window vivid and calm
As though composed in a rigid water
No random traffic would dispel . . .

As now through the park, and across
The chill nailed colors of the roofs,
And on near trees stripped bare,

Corrected in the scant remaining leaf
To their severe essential elegance,
Light is the all-exacting good,

That dry, forever virile stream
That wipes each thing to what it is,
The whole, collage and stone, cleansed
To its proper pastoral . . .
                                        I sit
And smoke, and linger out desire.

And know if I closed my eyes I'd hear
Again what held me awake all night
Beside her breathing: a rain falling
It seemed into a distant stillness,
On broad low leaves beside a pond
And drop upon drop into black waters.

I cannot recall any other poem by Alvin that is this celebratory, though a cleansing light is the entire basis for rejoicing. When I first read "November Sunday Morning," actually handed to me by the poet on a Sunday morning just before Thanksgiving, it renewed memories of my youth, when I would wander round our neighborhood early in the day and experience instant clarification of streets grown too drearily familiar. I had no name then for these bursts of transcendence, nor did they move me to composition, since any desire to write poems was alien to me. Poetry was what I read incessantly, possessed by memory, and wanted to absorb gradually. The genesis of a literary critic, at least in me, was remote from any incarnation of the poetical character.

"November Sunday Morning" is a hymn to light and reminds me that Alvin enjoyed chanting aloud Milton's invocation to book III of *Paradise Lost*. Milton and Wordsworth were his favorites among the major English poets. I remarked once to my friend that he did not center upon the sun as did Walt Whitman and Wallace Stevens but only upon the light. It was as if his sense of natural light cut itself off from the solar trajectory in defiance of Nietzsche's Zarathustra and of all poets who emerged from Nietzsche's shadow. What mattered about the light for Alvin was its cleansing effect upon everything open to perception. Plato would not have termed the light an all-exacting good, yet Feinman was no Platonist. Severe and rigorous, "November Sunday Morning" offers only a self-limiting transcendence. That so minimal a vision should become a poem of this extraordinary distinction continues to surprise me after so many decades of repeated recitations that I murmur to myself in the small hours of the night.

I remember Alvin's attachment to Pilgrim Heights on Cape Cod. When first he showed me this poem I remarked it could take a Stevensian title: "I Was Myself the Compass of That Sea":

Pilgrim Heights

Something, something, the heart here
Misses, something it knows it needs
Unable to bless—the wind passes;
A swifter shadow sweeps the reeds,
The heart a colder contrast brushes.

So this fool, face-forward, belly
Pressed among the rushes, plays out
His pulse to the dune's long slant
Down from blue to bluer element,
The bold encompassing drink of air

And namelessness, a length compound
Of want and oneness the shore's mumbling
Distantly tells—something a wing's
Dry pivot stresses, carved
Through barrens of stillness and glare:

The naked close of light in light,
Light's spare embrace of blade and tremor
Stealing the generous eye's plunder
Like a breathing banished from the lung's
Fever, lost in parenthetic air.

Raiding these nude recesses, the hawk
Resumes his yielding balance, his shadow
Swims the field, the sands beyond,
The narrow edges fed out to light,
To the sea's eternal licking monochrome.

The foolish hip, the elbow bruise
Upright from the dampening mat,
The twisted grasses turn, unthatch,
Light-headed blood renews its stammer—
Apart, below, the dazed eye catches

A darkened figure abruptly measured
Where folding breakers lay their whites;
The heart from its height starts downward,
Swum in that perfect pleasure
It knows it needs, unable to bless.

Feinman's almost solipsistic rapture partly is inherited from Stevens's Whitmanian Hoon, who finds himself more truly and more strange by singing another Song of Myself. When he gave me the poem I initially felt wonder at what seemed Alvin's most distinguished performance up to that time. After more than sixty years the sense of ecstasy that for him constituted the spirit of solitude has become more dialectical in my understanding. The darkened figure who breaks the poet's reverie restores the shadow of an external world. Feinman balances the perfect pleasure that the poetic heart requires against the cost of confirmation that is a stance excluding the power of blessing otherness, whether in persons or in the hawk's yielding balance. The poem labors to attain a generosity toward otherness and yet knowingly falls short of this accomplishment.

William Butler Yeats, another presence haunting Feinman's poetry, trusted that casting out remorse would give him a sense of being blessed by everything and then looking upon all otherness and blessing it. Feinman, who comes later, has a vision of the mind as a ceaseless activity, engaged in suffering a process of working apart all things that are joined by it. That rending allows no hope of being blessed even by the mind's power over a universe of death.

Alvin's major poem is "Preambles," a hard, driving gamble with the limits of discursiveness. Its opening never abandons my memory:

Vagrant, back, my scrutinies
The candid deformations as with use

A coat or trouser of one now dead
Or as habit smacks of certitude

Even cosmographies, broad orchards
The uncountable trees   Or a river
Seen along the green monotonies
Of its banks   And the talk

Of memorable ideals ending
In irrelevance   I would cite
Wind-twisted spaces, absence
Listing to a broken wall

Though it is a poem in three parts, each segment flows without break, a quality that adds to the difficulty of discussing individual passages. Thus the montage of "Wind-twisted spaces, absence / Listing to a broken wall" leads on to further wounded tropes:

And the cornered noons
Our lives played in, such things
As thwart beginnings, limit   Or
Juxtapose that longest vision

A bright bird winged to its idea
To the hand stripped
By a damaged resolution
Daily of its powers   *Archai*

Bruited through crumbling masteries
To hang like swollen apples
In the river, witnesses
Stilled to their clotted truth   All

Discursion fated and inept
So the superior reality
Of photographs   The soul's
Tragic abhorrence of detail.

I hear in the foreground of this the aura of Hart Crane's "Repose of Rivers" and a shadow of his "Sunday Morning Apples," a poem Alvin liked to recite to me. Yet Crane does not present us with the cognitive difficulties that are the matrix of "Preambles." Memory in Hart Crane transmembers the poet's sufferings into song, but in Feinman memory is always blocked. His scrutinies return to him damaged by their overreaching and yield him metaphors of deformation, twisting, absence, thwarting, limiting, stripping, and clotting. The image of working apart what has been inextricably and exquisitely joined is his central trope.

In the second preamble an adagio intervenes, as if to lower the poem's intolerable tension, though the darkness gathers and does not fall:

> So
> Statues hold through every light
> The grave persuasive
>
> Candors of their stride   And so
> The mind in everything it joins
> And suffers to redeem apart
> Plays victim to its own intent

Wallace Stevens in his "Saint John and the Back-Ache" has the Back-Ache, which I take to be the fallen history of each of us, complain to Saint John:

> The mind is the terriblest force in the world, father,
> Because, in chief, it, only, can defend
> Against itself. At its mercy, we depend
> Upon it.

I recall remarking to Alvin in 1955, while we toured Devon and Cornwall together, that Stevens had a premonition of the impasse "Preambles" was to constitute for the later poet. The final section of Feinman's major poem renders that impasse with an agile but self-undoing eloquence:

> These even love's rejoinder
> As of every severed thing
>
> The *ecce* only, only hands
> Or hardnesses, the gleam a water
> Or a light, a paused thing
> Clothes in vacua killed
>
> To a limbless beauty   Take
> These torn possessives there

Where you plead the radiant
Of your truth's gloom   Own

To your sleep, your waking
The tread that is walked
From the inner of its pace
The play of a leaf to an earth.

The image of severing always negates the gleams and radiances
that Feinman ultimately inherited from Wordsworth and from Ste-
vens. For Wordsworth the light of common day at last subsumed
the glory and the freshness of his poetic dream. Stevens, who cried
out jubilantly: "What is there here but weather, what spirit / Have
I except it comes from the sun?," sustained his poetry in Whitman's
mode of opening the self to the wind and the weather and, above
all, the sun. I sorrowed even in the middle 1950s that Alvin was
destroying his extraordinary gift by an asceticism alien to poetic
vision.

I do not find in any of the new poems in this volume anything
equal to the best work in the book I helped to foster, *Preambles
and Other Poems* (1964). The only one that moves me greatly
is "Matinal," initially titled "Morning-Hymn for the Breaker of
Horses." I have no idea when Alvin composed this, and at first
reading it seemed a kind of self-parody. Gradually I have come to
admire it, but with some reservations, since its high style is rather
hyperbolical. Feinman must have been aware that W. B. Yeats is
too strong a presence in "Matinal."

Where wild god-bridled terrors joy
My thundered pulse; not I,
Some lashed stone presence wakes
To wield, to quicken, buoy
This thrill galvanic gusto sky-
Ward where sun-slashed heavens break,

To chant the reins of spirit skilled
To bone, as is thy sling
Of brilliance turmoil bound,
Thy mounted salvos drilled
Past dare of conjuring
The paean of tempest deafness drowned:

Alvin was always happiest on or near rocky beaches, whether on Cape Cod or in Cornwall. He particularly liked to watch dawn come up, and exulted in the impact of wave on rock. His ascetic spirit was assuaged by the blast and vaulting of the wind's voice echoing cliffs and scattering the light of a new day. Seven years after his final vanishing, I continue to mourn both my friend and the gift he failed to nurture. I write this in the elegy season of early November 2015, and end this celebratory foreword with the final quatrain of "Matinal":

> Wave shattering wave, past sense,
> Past power commute the breath,
> O epic tempo of no birth or death
> Blastbind the blood thy reverence.

Corrupted into Song

The Constant Crime of Speech

THE LIFE AND WORK OF ALVIN FEINMAN

By James Geary

When Alvin Feinman arrived at Bennington College as a literature instructor in the fall of 1969 he was not yet 40 but, to students, already seemed immensely old. His face was lined and grave, his teeth yellowed by nicotine stains, his voice sonorous and low, with deep Old Testament overtones.

Everything about him was solemn, deliberate, slow. A brooding presence at the seminar table, he sat with two Styrofoam cups before him, one for black coffee and one for ash. After reading aloud a line of poetry, he took a long, melancholic drag on his Parliament and waited, in silence, for what felt like ages.

Harold Bloom and John Hollander recommended Alvin to Bennington's Literature and Languages Division. Alvin and Bloom were inseparable during their grad school days at Yale in the 1950s, and Hollander was a fierce and early admirer of what was at the time Alvin's only book, *Preambles and Other Poems*, published in 1964. Alvin had done some sporadic teaching—at Queens College, Brooklyn College and Yale—but spent most of the previous decade writing and editing documentary films in lower Manhattan.

His teaching method came not from years of lecturing, but from a total devotion to poetry. Alvin taught as he read: painstakingly, meticulously, utterly. "His way of speaking about poetry seemed like something so basic to human experience," says Vivian Heller, who studied with Alvin from 1972 through 1976 and was his Literature and Languages Division colleague from 1988 to 1994. "It was not an intellectual exercise, but like life itself, as deep and irreducible as nature, an essential form of human expression."

Students revered Alvin for his forensic reading. He never got through more than half a syllabus, if that, during a semester, and tales of his immersive attention to individual words and phrases are legion. In one Milton class, he gave a two-hour disquisition on the philosophical implications of the prefix "dis" in *Paradise Lost*. In the Poetics course I took with him in 1984, he spent two weeks dissecting a single line from one of Pindar's *Odes*. In his Romanticism class, he introduced the concept by devoting several sessions to the anonymous sixteenth-century English lyric "Western Wind," which reads in its entirety:

Western wind, when will thou blow,
The small rain down can rain?
Christ! If my love were in my arms,
And I in my bed again!

Alvin slowed things down. He wasn't finished with a poem until every line, every word was scrutinized, every punctuation mark felt. A student review of a 1972 Romanticism class, written by Ted Mooney, now a novelist and short story writer, begins, "All agree that the course continued at a snail's pace, and that, as before, we dined occasionally on escargot for our pains. Which is to say that the substance of the course has been indefinite, insight occurring rather than accumulating; it's hard to know where we have arrived. But the flashes along the way have been more than valuable, and the trouble to weave them together seems worth the taking."

The pace was glacial, but after Alvin's attention receded students found new depths and details glittering across a poem's surface. "You owed the work your best effort, your best self," is how Christina Rago, who studied at Bennington from 1970 to 1974 and was a member of that 1972 Romanticism class, describes Alvin's pedagogy. "The respect you give the poem is your full and compete attention and all of your critical acumen. That's what made the classroom come alive."

Kathy Halbreich, who attended Bennington from 1967 to 1971, says simply, "Alvin taught me to read."

The mystique surrounding Alvin's own work was as compelling as his Talmudic teaching methods. "Students felt he was special," says Barbara Smith, who taught at Bennington from 1960 to 1973, of her Literature and Languages Division colleague, "that he represented the highest quality of poetry making."

Preambles was regarded on campus with a mixture of apprehension and awe. The poems are metaphysically dense and can be daunting, but the language and lyricism are ravishing. Alvin was reticent about his own work, though, and didn't publish again until *Preambles* was reissued, along with a handful of additional poems, in 1990. Why the 26-year silence? Was Alvin still writing? Everyone wondered; few dared ask. Though Alvin had not a trace of pretension or hauteur, there was something forbidding about him, a quality Daniel Myerson, a student in the early 1970s, experienced as "vatic irritability."

As a person, Alvin was inscrutable. Incapable of small talk, he rarely invited socializing outside the classroom, on a campus known for the relaxed interaction between students and faculty. He was never rude or unkind—on the contrary, he had a grand, Old World gallantry—but could nevertheless come across as unapproachable.

Alvin always kept himself slightly removed, standing a little off to the side of life. Though he was a regular at the Wednesday night poker games held, among others, at sculptor Willard Boepple's house on the grounds of the Park-McCullough mansion in North Bennington during the 1970s, novelist Nicholas Delbanco, who taught at Bennington from 1969 to 1985, remembers Alvin as "a little withdrawn and bemused. The company of men with cigars and cognac was not his element."

Among the game's other fixtures were novelist Bernard Malamud, artists Jules Olitski and Kenneth Noland, composer Lou Calabro, and Danny Fager, who owned the gas station just off campus, with occasional appearances by former Bennington president Frederick Burkhardt and television producer Norman Lear. Tommy Ollendorff, who attended Bennington from 1969 to 1971, joined as a fluke one night when the regulars were down a man. He ended up playing most of his senior year, usually sitting next to Alvin. "He was childlike and otherworldly, even though he had tremendous gravitas," Ollendorff recalls, "always looking at things a plane above the game, marveling at it like a child in a planetarium."

To get near enough to ask Alvin if he was still writing was a fearsome task. The closest I ever came was during a discussion of Hart Crane that took place at one of our weekly student-advisor meetings. I worked with Alvin on my senior thesis, a collection of original poems and aphorisms plus an essay on Crane's poetry. I said something about how tragic Crane's suicide was because it deprived us of the great poetry he would have written had he lived. "I'm not so sure," was Alvin's stark reply. I understood him to mean that Crane was already spent as a poet when he took his own life, his best and only worthwhile work already behind him. I couldn't help but think, then as now, that Alvin was also speaking of himself.

The son of Litvak Jews who emigrated to the United States before World War I from an area of Eastern Europe now comprising parts of Lithuania, Belarus, Latvia, Poland, and Ukraine, Alvin Feinman was born on November 21, 1929, in the East New York area of Brooklyn. He was the youngest of five siblings, the only boy. Yiddish was spoken at home. His father, Morris, manufactured console radios and prospered during the 1920s, tooling around town in a Duesenberg. But then the Crash came, as did portable radios, and the family's fortunes turned.

Morris found work in the garment industry and fished on weekends in the Atlantic off Far Rockaway, bringing home sea bass, porgies, croakers, and blowfish. Richard Halpern, Morris's grandson and Alvin's nephew, recalls fishing with his grandfather as a boy into the early 1950s: "He was a mystic when it came to fishing, always catching dozens of fish even when others caught nothing."

Alvin's mother, Frieda, raised her five children amidst the stresses of sudden poverty. The family managed to keep their own house throughout the Depression, but they lost their comparatively affluent lifestyle and were often without heat and hot water. Morris's mystical angling ability kept them—and much of the neighborhood—supplied with fish. Alvin's oldest sister, Sylvia, known as Tibby, remembers her mother concocting an amazing variety of fish dishes during those lean years. She also remembers Frieda spending about a month one summer at a hotel in the Catskills. The children were told a doctor had said their mother needed "a change of scene," but Tibby guesses she was suffering from depression.

Litvak scholars are known for their interrogative, intellectual approach to Talmud study, and Alvin came from a long line of rabbis. His grandfather, Avram, was a particularly imposing figure.

"People straightened up when he walked down the street," according to Halpern. It was said of Rabbi Avram that if you put your finger on any spot on the cover of the Pentateuch, he could tell you every word on every page below that spot throughout all five books.

Similar things were said about Alvin and his sacred scripture, Milton. Quote any line from *Paradise Lost*, students said, and Alvin could recite the full passage. And like his grandfather, Alvin had an invigorating effect on those around him. "So much of Alvin was his presence," says Maura Spiegel, a Literature and Languages Division faculty member from 1984 to 1992. "He created his own atmosphere. Every discussion went up a notch. You sensed he was made of different stuff."

Students wanted some of that stuff to rub off on them. I remember loitering one day near the top of the stairs in The Barn, the old red farm building where literature classes are held, as Alvin passed. He stopped in front of me and asked, somewhat abruptly, "What are you waiting for?" I skipped a beat and said, "They also serve who only stand and wait." He grinned and walked away. To be smiled upon by Alvin was a high honor.

Behind his intimidating exterior, Alvin had a wry, idiosyncratic sense of humor, theorizing, for example, that cats devolved from human beings by choice. When Alvin did choose to socialize, he and Deborah Dorfman, his partner of more than 50 years, who died in the summer of 2015, were gracious, convivial hosts, entertaining faculty colleagues and former students at their home for lunch. In conversation, Alvin was always alert to the nuances and ramifications of language. A billboard advertising "Self Storage" prompted an ontological consideration of whether such a thing was even possible; and, during one Sunday afternoon lunch, when Spiegel's three-year-old was whining at the table, Alvin quipped, "What oft was Thought, but ne'er so well Exprest."

Alvin graduated in 1951 with a BA in philosophy from Brooklyn College. One of his classmates was the writer Carl Solomon, to whom Allen Ginsberg dedicated *Howl*. The Beat movement was starting to happen all around him, but Alvin did not take part. His austere, ascetic verse has little in common with the Whitmanesque exuberance of the Beats. From Brooklyn College he went to Yale, where he spent the next six years, apart from stints at the University of Chicago and the University of Heidelberg on a Fulbright. He completed his MA in philosophy but never finished his dissertation, on Kierkegaard, so never received a doctorate. It was largely at Yale that Alvin wrote the poems in *Preambles* as well as the poems published for the first time in this volume.

Yale wanted Alvin to join its faculty but had to let him go because he chose not to complete his PhD, a requirement to teach there. So, in 1957 he moved back to New York City, where he worked a variety of odd jobs. He and Dorfman, also a Yale grad student, spent a lot of time in the cafes, bookstores, and record shops of Greenwich Village and Chelsea. Any money Alvin had went to phonograph records to feed his omnivorous appetite for music. He listened obsessively to everything—opera, early music, blues, liturgical hymns, bluegrass—except rock and pop.

He eventually found a job writing and editing documentary films, where he met the jovial, outgoing Jerry Michaels, an aspiring artist who had worked as an assistant to photographer Helen Levitt, known for her images of the New York City streets, and author, screenwriter, and film critic James Agee. The two became close friends, despite their seemingly mismatched characters. Where Alvin was taciturn and morose, Michaels was voluble and jolly; where Alvin was rabbinic, Michaels was Rabelaisian. Michaels had an encyclopedic block-by-block knowledge of New York City, and he and Alvin spent hours walking around town, Alvin delighting in the historical and architectural details Michaels pointed out.

Apart from Michaels, Alvin had few friends and a minimal social life during the decade or so he lived in Lower Manhattan. He saw Dorfman, who was teaching in California and upstate New York, only occasionally, and only rarely visited his family.

During the summer of 1963, when Alvin was finalizing the manuscript of Preambles, Halpern, then a junior in college, visited his uncle several times a week. They took walks around the neighborhood, ate frogs' legs at Café Normandy and steak at the Old Homestead Steak House on Ninth Avenue. Alvin was—uncharacteristically—avuncular, urging Halpern to learn a trade, get a PhD, and master at least one foreign language.

At some point, Alvin's mental state veered into darker psychological terrain. He and Dorfman talked on the phone late at night, Alvin confiding that he felt he was losing his grip on reality. He stopped showing up for work, and not even strolls with Jerry Michaels could rouse him. "He spent years in his room listening to music," Dorfman said of this period. Bloom remembers Alvin at this time as "contemplative, cut off from life, mostly being alone, reflecting in a state of almost mystical contemplation."

When *Preambles* appeared, luminaries like Bloom, Conrad Aiken, Allen Tate, and R.W.B. Lewis praised the book, but broader critical recognition was scant. Hayden Carruth, in an otherwise unflattering 1965 note in *The Hudson Review* ("The poems are difficult; some are so difficult that they are laughable"), did alight on one important insight: "His poems are an apparent attempt to give affective form to real metaphysical torment."

Metaphysical torment was something many colleagues and students sensed. "On some level, Alvin was in despair," Barbara Smith says. "There was a morbid side to him. He would often see an unhappy, fatal aspect to things."

That fatality was there in his world-weary detachment from the mundane offices of everyday life, in the distance he was careful to keep between himself and others, in his pessimistic stance that the world was too much with us. Alvin was walking through Bennington's Commons building on May 10, 1994, as a group of students watched Nelson Mandela's inauguration as South African president on television. He paused, recited Yeats's "Parnell"—"Parnell came down the road, he said to a cheering man: / 'Ireland shall get her freedom and you still break stone'"—and moved on. Fatalism is there in his own poetry, too, in the sense of resignation that language would never do everything he wanted it to.

In the late 1960s, when Alvin was ready to return to the world, he picked up teaching again. His friend, philosopher Richard Rorty, arranged an evening course at Queens College. He also taught a survey of English lit at C.W. Post College on Long Island. When Bloom and Hollander suggested Bennington, he somewhat reluctantly agreed. "Alvin wanted to be alone, to steer out of the way of the complications of real life," Bloom says, "but teaching saved him by forcing him out."

Somewhat to his own surprise, Alvin quickly took to small-town life in Vermont, developing a genuine passion for gardening. He loved showing off his garden to visitors, often dispensing advice as he walked. During a visit in the early 1980s, he showed Christina Rago and Sam Schulman (the latter was part of the first cohort of males to be admitted to the college in the late 1960s) how to pop peony roots out of the ground with a shovel and cut them in half for better flowering. With mock ceremony, he then presented them with root stock descended from a peony planted by Robert Frost at Shingle Cottage, a Bennington faculty house where both poets lived for a time during their respective tenures at the college.

Bloom, who still recites "November Sunday Morning," "Stare at the Sea," and "Pilgrim Heights" to himself when he can't sleep, chided Alvin that he was "replacing poems with eggplants." Bloom says Alvin's response to those entreaties to resume writing poetry was "just silence."

Alvin avoided anything that smacked of "the racket," as he called it, the academic niceties incumbent upon college professors. He did not attend conferences, did not publish in literary journals, did not bring out a new collection of poems every couple of years. In a verse reflection, composed around the same time as the poems in *Preambles*, which reads as a defense of both his poetry and his Bartleby-like preference for avoiding professional obligations, he wrote:

> I have nothing to say
> to the concept of yourself you enact
> in the professionalisms of the world you have been sold
> or inherited, or assumed to be a world.
> . . .
> What good is truth if it can be told
> only by those who spend their days
> in libraries, who take nine miles
> of small-print syllogisms, infested with footnotes
> as with dazed lice, to have their say.

Alvin was even skeptical of creative writing workshops, a mainstay of Bennington's emphasis on learning by doing. He took the view that, if you wanted to be a poet, you should be reading Milton and Wordsworth, not the poems of your classmates.

Alvin probably only ever gave one reading, during his first year at Bennington, most likely in the spring of 1970. Among his manuscripts are notes for planned remarks that day, along with a running order of titles. He had excluded some of the poems on the list—"The Way to Remember Her," "Stanzas for W. B. Yeats," "Stone Anatomies," among others—from *Preambles*, though the fact that he apparently included them in this reading suggests he still valued them.

The reading notes, scrawled in a large hand across the page, seem meant to address the accusations of "difficulty" made by Carruth and encountered by others in *Preambles*. This difficulty, Alvin wrote, was "experimental or committed to an idea of the essence of poetry," which involved the use of language "prior to (more interior than) anything we have to say; i.e., our very wish itself to speak."

> Perhaps up to a point in life: there is our overall sense of self, of world (always partly unformed) and of language/words as obscurely mediating between them but perhaps <u>falsely</u> committing us when we utter them or that they (we, the world) are always compromised into an over-concrete version of each. So the thing would be to say (if one could hear) what <u>language/speech itself wished to say</u> (its own "intentionality") prior to use (abuse) as sign, where it wanted to go, that poetry in its essence draws on this pure potency of language not simply as sound but that behind the word is the idea of the word, that in this poetry defends us against the world (fixity–already knownness) and our own egotism, willfulness, our loss of, corruption of meaning: so poetry purges us of the constant crime of speech.

This purgative is at work in "The Way to Remember Her," an incantatory lyric that is the photographic negative of a conventional love poem. Instead of counting the ways the loved one is beloved, these very details—hand, lips, eyes, flower—are whited out by exposure to imaginative light. In accordance with the poem's list of stern imperatives—"take," "dispel," "tear"—and the thrice-repeated demand to "burn the name of it," one by one specifics are expunged, until in the end only a luminous outline of the beloved remains. The poem's key command is "imagine, do not look," affirming that passion's true and only souvenir is not what hands or lips have touched but what occurs to and in the mind. Hence, the final stanza:

—Or burn that hand, the lips,
The eyes, the flower, all, all save
The knowledge, the desire that kills
And leaves the burning name of it.

For Alvin, the "crime of speech" lay in committing experience to language that was not true to its essence. His high ambition for poetry was not that it describe or approximate experience but that it *be* experience. "For a poet, it is never a matter of saying *it is raining*," Paul Valéry wrote. "It's a matter of . . . making rain."

In one of Alvin's copies of *Preambles*, I found a sheet of paper with two quotations scribbled on it, one from R. P. Blackmur and one from Geoffrey Moore. Alvin wrote "of W.S." (perhaps William Shakespeare) at the top of the sheet. The Moore quote reads: "One has a sense while reading him that creation is proceeding before one's eyes. The whole is a continuous process, not a 'talking about' . . . so that, one receives through the aesthetic sense an impression of pure potency." Alvin underlined the excerpt in pencil up through "talking about," then underlined that same passage again in red pencil.

Alvin used the phrase "pure potency" in the notes for his reading, and his poems convey the same sense Moore describes of creation taking place before one's very ears and eyes. "The Way to Remember Her," as so many of Alvin's poems, is an account of an intense emotional, even spiritual experience that catalyzes a similar experience in the reader. These poems are "difficult" because saying what language/speech itself wishes to say is difficult. The process is the poem, and vice versa. The great challenge and reward of Alvin's poems is that in reading them one participates in their making.

Apart from his foreword in this volume, Harold Bloom's consideration of Alvin's work in *The Ringers in the Tower*, published in 1971, is still the only sustained critical treatment the poems have received. "Though thoroughly justifiable, the difficulty is pre-amble to Feinman's failure to make a canon of poems, to the slow waste of his genius," Bloom writes. "Though there are parallel problems in consciousness in Valéry and Rilke, those poets fortu-nately were free of the peculiarly American malady of seeking to be Ananke [ancient Greek personification of necessity or fate], which in Feinman's case becomes the deplorable quest to write the last possible poem, a work that takes the post-Romantic con-sciousness so far as to make further advances in self-consciousness intolerable."

There is throughout Alvin's poetry a keen awareness that fur-ther advance is not only intolerable but impossible, that coming to the end of the mind he found not a palm but a brick wall. His greatest poems—"Pilgrim Heights," "November Sunday Morn-ing," and "Preambles" itself—are preliminary, pre-ambulatory, in that they take as their starting point the impossibility of even be-ginning. This dilemma is repeatedly restated—"all discursion fated and inept," "The helpless span narration cannot close," "such things as thwart beginnings"—but never resolved. Each foray to find the source of that "pure potency" culminates in a dead end, as in the last two lines of "L'Impasse des Deux Anges," where two figures are locked in a contest in which neither can prevail:

Regard these two, perpetual, firm,
Closed in a struggle that cannot bend.

Bloom recalls that Alvin was as unbending as the figures in "L'Impasse des Deux Anges." "Alvin felt that he wouldn't achieve the absolute poem, and that's all he wanted to have done," he says of his conversations with Alvin about his work. "The rest would have been proliferation. That's what made him magnificent and, in the end, self-destructive as a poet. We lost lots of very fine poetry because of Alvin's curious attitude."

Alvin's attitude may seem less curious in light of how he himself appears to have regarded his work. In another of his copies of *Pre-ambles*, I found several sheets of paper with jottings that parallel the notes he made for his Bennington reading. At the top of one sheet, "q. of difficulty" (question of difficulty) is underlined in red pencil and below it are the words "tempt. to lect., expl., or apologize (since poetry is a crime)." Alvin had no difficulty resisting the temptation to lecture on or explain his work, and he certainly never apologized for it. To do so would, in fact, have been to reduce the poems to the fixed, overly concrete meanings he thought inherently false. "He believed real poetry cannot be fully reduced or resolved," says Vivian Heller. "It was not what a line 'meant' that was important but what it suggested or evoked. He didn't like things to be pinpointed in the end."

Just below the line about lecturing and explaining, Alvin wrote: "Poetry itself a compromise with ineffable." Perhaps Alvin chose not to produce new work because he was unwilling to compromise or no longer able to, as he wrote in "Day, Daylong," "enter speech that does not speak / Consent, and claim, and failure to conclude."

The manuscripts show that Alvin stopped making new poems before the publication of *Preambles*, with one exception—"Second Marriage Song," the final piece in *Poems*, dedicated to his friends Jane Sobel and Stanley Rosen, dated "Thanksgiving Day, 1987 / North Bennington, Vermont." But Alvin never stopped writing, never stopped thinking and rethinking his poems.

During the late 1980s, John Hollander had been prodding Alvin for another book. It was around this time that students in Alvin's poetry workshop were startled when, during a discussion of the revision process, he produced a copy of "November Sunday Morning" from his pocket and proceeded to read it aloud.

In preparing *Preambles* for publication in 1963, Dorfman had persuaded Alvin to remove the last stanza from the original poem, so it ended with "I sit / And smoke, and linger out desire." In *Poems*, he restored the missing last stanza, explaining in a draft of a February 1989 letter to Bloom: "I have thought the restored last stanza at least activates a premise that complicates the 'genre' (toward Resolution & Independence: the opening frame)."

Alvin also read aloud "Second Marriage Song" in class. "Hearing him read in his quiet, powerful, resonant voice, no one spoke, no one moved," recalls Shay Totten, who was in the workshop that day. "He didn't stop smoking, ever, so he was holding a cigarette the whole time, the ash getting longer and longer. There was a sense that this was really something special he just shared with us."

For *Poems*, Alvin inserted two pieces—"This Tree" and "Death of the Poet"—into the original *Preambles* sequence and changed the title of "What Land" to "What Speaking Silent Enough?" Apart from "Second Marriage Song," the ten other additional poems appended to the end of *Preambles* were all written at the same time as that work, in the mid- to late 1950s.

The revisions Alvin made to some of those poems show the meticulousness of his attention and that, in some ways, he hadn't finished writing them. In "Snow," he added the word "now" to the end of the second line in the final stanza. He changed the break in the next-to-last line of "Relic," as he did in the third line of "For the Child Unanswered in Her." In "Responsibilities and Farewell," he replaced the original "stunned" in the third line with "strung" and deleted the entire tenth line.

In *The Ringers in the Tower*, Bloom writes, "like Crane, [Alvin] is wholly a visionary, but afflicted (unlike Crane) with a critical consciousness in the mode of Valéry. He cannot create by dissociation, but only by joinings, like Whitman and Crane, joinings to which nevertheless he cannot give credence." In Alvin's poems, two aspects of mind are at work: one that writes and by writing tries to unite, and another that picks apart the very things the poem tries to connect. This constant stitching and unstitching—"the vacant / Presence of unjoined necessary things," "soul's torn two intellects," "the one footfall that bruises us asunder"—gives the poems a tidal feel. They repeatedly approach a kind of unity or closure, but inevitably recede just before reaching it. From "Preambles":

> The mind in everything it joins
> And suffers to redeem apart
> Plays victim to its own intent.

The mind sometimes sidesteps its own victimhood, though, most notably in "Backyard, Hoboken, Summer" and "Summer, Afternoon," two of the very few of Alvin's poems that can be described as celebratory.

Both poems are relatively straightforward depictions of summer days: "a cat slouching on the woodpile / And flies nauseous with heat," "the string / of ducks drawn through the pond." What's different is that the intellect at work here is not torn or dissecting, nor are the scenes rendered in such sensual detail sundered from the viewer or the writer. On the contrary, it is "As though within the clot of brain / Were space or sun to make a world" and "The comfort of this ground / Is physical: the sun / Goes through your shirt like liniment."

These poems go through your brain like liniment, suffusing an intensity and warmth that anneals—for a moment, at least—the rupture so many of Alvin's other poems probe. In "Pilgrim Heights," which takes place in a similar summer setting, the heart misses something, something "It knows it needs, unable to bless." In "Backyard, Hoboken, Summer" and "Summer, Afternoon," the heart relents, blesses, and in so doing finds that "pure potency" where words are the fitting and authentic medium for world. Alvin once said the task of poetry was to "get back to the pre-interpreted world." These two poems do just that: "nothing / Here is not enough to be without / All need to ever argue for."

In his 1972 Romanticism class, Alvin defined the movement's central insight and innovation as "the apprehension of the activity of the mind in constituting its world and its surroundings. The poet is consciousness that the mind creates the scene that it views." This consciousness both blesses and curses: blesses because it meshes the writing mind with the world it seeks to create, the reading of a poem with the making of it; and curses because it requires of the poet a difficult double role—to be both participant in and observer of the creative process, a task described in "Stare at the Sea":

> Teach the sea to sing, the soul
> To drink its own imagining.

If the poet plays both roles well, perhaps the poem gets behind the word to the idea of the word. If not, there is always silence, as in "True Night":

> As long as truest night is long,
> Let no discordant wing
> Corrupt these sorrows into song.

In 1994, Alvin, along with about a third of Bennington's other faculty, was dismissed from the college. During the previous year, then president Elizabeth Coleman and the Board of Trustees had begun a process to re-evaluate the college's future, convinced that Bennington faced financial and pedagogical challenges that threatened its continued existence. The recommendations they published in June of 1994 included, among other measures, the dissolution of academic divisions in favor of faculty working groups and the abolition of the college's presumptive tenure system. At the end of the month, some two dozen teachers, including Alvin, were dismissed.

The American Association of University Professors condemned the dismissals as an attack on academic freedom. A group of terminated faculty filed a lawsuit against Bennington, arguing that they were dismissed because they opposed Coleman's plans for the college. In December of 2000, the case was settled out of court; fired faculty received $1.89 million in compensation and an apology from Bennington.

According to Dorfman, Alvin was furious at Coleman's and the Board's actions but equally appalled by the polarization the dispute provoked among faculty. Though he was a vocal opponent of Coleman's plans and sparred with her at faculty meetings, he did not join his colleagues in the lawsuit. Amidst the uproar on campus, Alvin was soon faced with a different challenge: He was diagnosed with Parkinson's.

During the last few years of his life, Alvin listened intensively to the blues, a genre he had always loved, becoming something of an evangelist for the form. He kept a stack of Alan Lomax's *Southern Journey Vol. 3: 61 Highway Mississippi—Delta Country Blues, Spirituals, Work Songs and Dance Music* CDs at home, which he handed out to friends. He found the music of Robert Johnson especially compelling. Vincent Carey, his niece's husband, made monthly visits around this time, and he and Alvin would often sit together and listen to music. "If I only had one thing in the world to listen to, this is the voice I would choose," Carey recalls Alvin saying of Johnson.

With the blues, as with poetry, Alvin was interested only in primary texts. He didn't respond to later offshoots. In the voices of Johnson and of the individuals Lomax recorded on his travels through the South, Alvin may have heard that pure, original sound of language saying what it wished to say.

As the Parkinson's progressed, Alvin found movement and speech increasingly difficult. But he always took visitors on little tours of his garden, picking his way through the rows of tomatoes and cucumbers with a cane. Rosie Schaap, a student at Bennington from 1990 to 1994, visited in the summer of 2007, a year before Alvin died. Strolling around the garden, she was struck by how important gardening had become to him and how, she thought, in some ways he had come to believe "gardening was a more effective kind of poetry than poetry."

Schaap had taken Alvin's course on Blake and remembered a discussion of one of the proverbs from *The Marriage of Heaven and Hell*, "To create a little flower is the labor of ages." "Poetry is making, *poesis*," Schaap recalls Alvin saying in class. "In a garden, that is more literal. The amazing thing about being human is the ability to make things. Nothing is bigger than that act of creation."

After the garden tour and lunch, as Schaap prepared to leave, Alvin handed her a copy of *Southern Journey Vol. 3*.

Throughout these final years, Dorfman said Alvin was perfectly content clearing brush and listening to music. He discovered an old tree stump in the garden and was able to clear away the dirt to expose the roots, a hydra-like skein of twisted shapes and hollow passages. He took great pleasure in poking at it with his cane, chipping away at this exquisitely, unreasonably joined thing.

As his partner for more than 50 years, Dorfman had always been respectful of Alvin's distance and reluctant to raise potentially difficult issues with him. She was the interface between Alvin and the world, softening its roughest edges and dispatching its most prosaic tasks. "I did the taxes" is how she described this aspect of their relationship. "I was less demanding than I should have been." But once, when the Parkinson's medication had loosened him up a bit, she asked if Alvin had ever thought of starting a family or being a more traditional breadwinner. "No," he said, "I thought of nothing but poetry."

In July of 2008, Alvin's condition worsened. He was hospitalized, able to eat nothing but ice chips. He listened to Marian Anderson's version of "I Know That My Redeemer Liveth" from Handel's *Messiah*, Haydn's *Mass in Time of War*, Andreas Scholl singing English folk songs, some Vivaldi, John Jacob Niles, and bluegrass. When the doctors said there was nothing more they could do for him, Dorfman brought him home to die.

Arriving home, he asked his caregivers first to carry him to the porch so he could see the delphiniums. Inside, Dorfman read aloud passages from Ecclesiastes, her favorite book of the Bible, and recited the song from *Cymbeline*, Alvin repeating after her each line:

Fear no more the heat o' the sun,
Nor the furious winter's rages;
Thou thy worldly task hast done,
Home art gone, and ta'en thy wages:
Golden lads and girls all must,
As chimney-sweepers, come to dust.

After she read "Morning, Arraignment with Image" from *Poems*, Alvin asked, "Who wrote that?" Dorfman understood him to mean: The person who wrote that poem is already gone.

Alvin's last words were, "I'm past tense."

Preambles

I

Preambles

I

Vagrant, back, my scrutinies
The candid deformations as with use
A coat or trousers of one now dead
Or as habit smacks of certitude

Even cosmographies, broad orchards
The uncountable trees   Or a river
Seen along the green monotonies
Of its banks   And the talk

Of memorable ideals ending
In irrelevance   I would cite
Wind-twisted spaces, absence
Listing to a broken wall

And the cornered noons
Our lives played in, such things
As thwart beginnings, limit   Or
Juxtapose that longest vision

A bright bird winged to its idea
To the hand stripped
By a damaged resolution
Daily of its powers   *Archai*

Bruited through crumbling masteries
To hang like swollen apples
In the river, witnesses
Stilled to their clotted truth   All

Discursion fated and inept
So the superior reality
Of photographs   The soul's
Tragic abhorrence of detail.

II

Only, if then, the ordered state
The storied sentiment of rest
Of the child hand in the father's
Rigored, islands tethered

To complicit seas, and tempering
Winds to lull the will
To evidence, to the ripe profit
Of perfections, gardens

Rhyming the space we walk in
Harmony of season and design   So
Statues hold through every light
The grave persuasive

Candors of their stride   And so
The mind in everything it joins
And suffers to redeem apart
Plays victim to its own intent

Divines generics blooded
To its needs   The sculptor
Lending outward in his stroke
To each defeat a signature

The just reconnaissance
That even fruit, each excellence
Confirms its course   A leisure
As of sap or blood arrested

Only once and to the prime
Its issue vivifies   A sun
Luring the divisioned calms
The days extended under it.

III

But only loosed or salient
Out of this unbinding stream
The stain of dyings seen
On pavements and on blurted

Slopes of ground   As there
Where your farthest reach
Is lived of want or membership
The ranged and slackened traffics

Cease   A bird in mid-flight
Falls, let silence, hair
The credible of touch adventure
There   Or certain laughters

Freedoms and the heat
Of only arms and of the thighs
These even love's rejoinder
As of every severed thing

The *ecce* only, only hands
Or hardnesses, the gleam a water
Or a light, a paused thing
Clothes in vacua killed

To a limbless beauty   Take
These torn possessives there
Where you plead the radiant
Of your truth's gloom   Own

To your sleep, your waking
The tread that is walked
From the inner of its pace
The play of a leaf to an earth.

Old World Travelogue

Back and late the northern valleys
And the carved centers of the west
Pitiably risen in flat places,
Their space, their calendar, a name
Affixed to treaties, distinctly ending:

The last stop, the wide sense of the edge.
Even these sure and splendid differences
Will mimic them, the wiser seemings
Of an open south, a mystery of flesh
More real, and incommutable—

Still in those starks the lungs will stumble,
Start to a skyline's baffled summoning:
One who strays at a rubbled limit,
Leans to a river and river-lights,
Hair blown, the spell of bridges . . .

Spurned divisions that will not close,
Gather to a claim, let the will relent:
So streets encountered in a guileless sun,
Words shaped to their translated sense,
A life contrived in a warmer country.

Landscape (Sicily)

I have seen your steeples and your lands
Speared by awkward cactuses and long birds
Flatten your yellow stones, your worn mountains.

Surely where those hills spilled villages
Toward the sea I should have wanted
Savagery, a touch icier than physical sport;

But vegetation withered from a forest
Of inconclusive starts, memory only
Gathered to a shade in the sun-sorrowed square.

A shade, sun-struck, whose hold will cover
The play of boys in blood-red clothing
And call your seasons to a wall of flatted rhythms,

To a slow summit of retreating days, days
Like winds through given linen, through dust.
These green reductions of your ancient freedoms—

The stunted olive, the lizard fixed
In soundless grasses, your yellow stones
Rubbed by the moon, the moon-quelled beaches,

And all asceticisms grown separate, skilled
To plump intrinsic endings—the fig-tree's
Sudden, rounded fingers; history

At the close will cripple to these things:
A body without eyes, a hand, the vacant
Presence of unjoined, necessary things.

II

Pilgrim Heights

Something, something, the heart here
Misses, something it knows it needs
Unable to bless—the wind passes;
A swifter shadow sweeps the reeds,
The heart a colder contrast brushes.

So this fool, face-forward, belly
Pressed among the rushes, plays out
His pulse to the dune's long slant
Down from blue to bluer element,
The bold encompassing drink of air

And namelessness, a length compound
Of want and oneness the shore's mumbling
Distantly tells—something a wing's
Dry pivot stresses, carved
Through barrens of stillness and glare:

The naked close of light in light,
Light's spare embrace of blade and tremor
Stealing the generous eye's plunder
Like a breathing banished from the lung's
Fever, lost in parenthetic air.

Raiding these nude recesses, the hawk
Resumes his yielding balance, his shadow
Swims the field, the sands beyond,
The narrow edges fed out to light,
To the sea's eternal licking monochrome.

The foolish hip, the elbow bruise
Upright from the dampening mat,
The twisted grasses turn, unthatch,
Light-headed blood renews its stammer—
Apart, below, the dazed eye catches

A darkened figure abruptly measured
Where folding breakers lay their whites;
The heart from its height starts downward,
Swum in that perfect pleasure
It knows it needs, unable to bless.

The Sun Goes Blind

The sun goes blind against my hand,
I lay the blue surrender of a bay
Down the burning corner of my reach.

The clouds retard and turn and catch,
Their casuistries cannot detain
What monody I move them through.

I let one silent flank alone
Of grazing pine encroach upon
The helmed embankments of my air.

Nameless, some quick or yellow bird
Finds me too wide to thread to flight,
Too still from bough to fretful bough.

Earth presses me in cramped duress—;
It is too gross a weight to be
Withheld, to labor forth—

                       this
Weight itself of weightlessness.

Scene Recalled

How should I not have preferred
The flinted salt of occasion?

The stern
Adequation I required of my eye:

> A time
> Of gulls riding out,
> Of the tide going cold at my ankles;

> A scene
> Held tall as postponement,
> As authority printed to landscape.

You are not the first man who exacted
Of flight it ascend through his shoulder;

Through the copper of nightfall the silver.

Solstice

Instance, the fire
that is in these facts, the burning
bearing into every edge
across the calm that
bridges them
                    here
is it, the central all
slumped in the sun
breezing itself its mid-day fever

a spire
is off, or fraught
awash, no special
grass but flat and porch
                              and only
jackbird sulks in his tree
the fire of his silence in me.

Snow

Now sudden, or again, this easy
Quieter. You will know its fall
And what it lies on,
All, sign, metal, tar
One long and skeletal reductum

As, but warm, this side the pane
You purchase sense for.
But the gods give down
Chill unities, the pulver of an under-
Lying argument, assuager

Of nothing nameable: you know
The light snow holds and what
Its bodyable shape
Subdues, the gutter of all things
A virgin unison; and how

The glass that frames this waste
Of contour lames to blur
The baffled figure
To the drift he scurries through
—Blear hazarder. More bold,

The discrepant mind will break
The centrum of its loss, now
Sudden and again,
Mistake its signature, as though
Snow were its poem out of snow.

Waters

Sunlight stitching the water—
an oar silverly lifted.
And blue, and yellow, and red boats drift—
like pleasures in a mind that needs no center.

One and one
leaves scuff into the lake and stop
drily as swans exchange their motions.

Last year's leaves. And boys
—stopping and starting
among the new vague blazes of the trees,
yellow, and suggested green—have now
a stiffened squirrel hung upon a stick
and lower him
with the firm excitement of natural action

his quick and singular attentions, all
that green and ragged round of starts
slipped under sieving waters.

Waters (2)

Broad emptiness of waters watched
  dull slant of light
  the roused abeyances of earth

So Chinese paintings
  not correcting the world
  invoke world-absences

Importantly
  because a breathing serves these pauses
  as though we were alone
  all birds south
  our loyalties renewing.

Earth and Sorrows

Grasses like knives and drilled
By the roots strangled   The upward
Downward tearings, and the dread
Irresistible sucking at a bruised
Defenseless sex   This remorseless
Forcing of a sickened ecstasy
                                        Earth
In her sensible labors pouring
The green extorted oils   Giving
Past shame   Or weeping   Or rejoicing

Let the winds consider
If these be the flower of her sorrow.

III

Relic

I will see her stand
half a step back of the edge of some high place
or at a leafless tree in some city park
or seated with her knees toward me and her face turned
        toward the window

And always the tips of the fingers of both her hands
will pull or twist at a handkerchief
like lovely deadly birds at a living thing
trying to work apart something exquisitely, unreasonably
        joined.

Three Elementary Prophecies
1. For Departure

You will not want what gives this going speech
Only as loss the stay of it
Not the rhythm drained into its sense
Like a world surviving

Only as absence, as a silence touched
A thing out of the body gone, desire
Or a blood-accustomed dread

Nor seek a knowledge of this breach
A name of it, as love
The flawless metamorphosis of dying
Stilled to its idea

Or membered like presentiment or choice
To your days' held mine
A sentence, or the letter of a truth

Only this presence destined
As a weather from its source
Toward broad or violent unleashings
Fables of the suffered and the joined

The rest unnumbered and devoid
A wind that will not move or pass
Rain tangled to a ruin, to
A season's felled forgotten root.

2. For Passage

Think then the ruin of your thoughts, and where
The persistent blood beats still under them,
Of birds you cannot follow with your eye.

Think the dark and breeding thickets
Where lowly animals die, and over the gloom
Bright birds passing in the light:

"What is your life if not the flashed stroke
Of your meaning, of water
Hurled once or blindly against rock,

Your living laid to the pillow of its sleep
As windows close to the street's tumult,
To love's long minute and the lips . . ."

Nail your will to the yellow fallings
Of your days, as tragedies slip
Their herald warnings through their acts.

Own land and sky, all seeing suffering things,
Water riding water, wing and roof,
The rip and baggage of all your ways.

3. For Return

Far, the farthest exile, and the steed
You ride must paw the ground, riderless,
Death's resignation come to matter

To mercies walked from the same blue fulcrum
Where your powers impel you
Unobscured by necessary pities,
                              hungers
Come like numbered birds in the common air
And needs before they improvise their names

There love will touch where your energies begin
Where your hand asks you light from primary colors,
Assembles a mystery detained by sorrows

Like roofs the color of particular houses
And the logic of unexpected trees, love
Like sons will be far in the night
Close, as horses in the night, and welcome.

What Speaking Silent Enough?

What silence speaking enough—:
Salt arbors, Archangels of the sea
Have slipped through slow impendings
Past risen things (what speech within?)
Of terrible ripeness
Of wet defeatingness
(Is a dripping body *silent*?)
As the sea contains, if this were lived in the sea;
If this were life there illumined.

That Ground

What acid eats the blind clay smile,
The earth how far, pummeled
In soft rain odors.

Never will it be possible to illumine that ground,
But know how her breathing
Shapes the hapless arms of trees;

How hair exhumes a menace of boughs,
Unvisited radiants darkling in the leaf;

And the smile a voice abused in winds,
The lips made possible
In virtue of silence,
Of the new distance of the earth.

This Face of Love

Nor prospect, promise   solely such
Breathed honey   as in breathing
Clamps the lung   and lowers life
Into this death   the very dying
Meaning of that breath   that beats
To black and beating honey   in an air
Thrown knowledgeless   imageless
Or only the wet hair   across her eyes.

For the Child Unanswered in Her

What scene, what street you started from
Is not abolished:
Stairwell, day-rise, long intonation of rain and piano,
And the dreamt animal meadow—
All laid waste, even at hair's breadth pierceable.

Child-heart, the illegible promise
Is not delivered in natural thickness
Of star and belly-loam.

Here by consummate gravities
Walls that have done and nothing
Pleads entrance to the mother arm:

                    —O listen,
The splendid throat of every column
Aloud in the beating nipple.

Bridgelessly lit as the seed's leap,
Convene your gaze to the Mortal Brow
Always near, always unable to return your wish.

Relic (2)

Who can say we are wrong to fail the circuit of guesses—
For I enter for you the frail damage of these lights
(Dear one forgive a driven youth its steel forgeries).

What you desert now loses me haltingly,
Surely voyager where you are, and welcomed
To your trackless survival of eyes;

As by gracious rain, frail windows,
Your eyes' help for the bitter green of the leaves.

Relic (3)

Icarian instant O my love!
That, and the hell you are burned for—
Your inverted egypt of timelessness:
That the years are an endless arcade
Where horizon to horizon
The far-shot streamers of your fireworks
Never quite extinguish.

Responsibilities and Farewell

Final, irredeemable, all
Saw that, coming to themselves,
The elision, strung, and farewell.

All were entered, entrusted, spoken
To the end, cancelled.
                              Saw youth,
The secret ascetic, the gunner,
Broken of all littler love, taken—

Was it some fool head in a gutter,
Blanks, or peaces, secrets of old men—
A shoe, a hat, a yellow, or a bench;

Or the eye of the human survivor?

Wiped of all but the whole desire,
Welcomed to the least all-seeing pleasure.

The End of the Private Mind

The end of the private mind
was in stone, in such thrifty thicknesses
including the connections
including the bits
                          —That
was the letting of it, it was not
obscure, but public as nails, as
stains in a flock of summery gutters

The death of it was generous
as it lived, only silly, and yet
not sillier, for Care
like an empty sleeve . . .
                          For Care,
a shy grass quiet in the cracks.

This Tree

Earth feeds him insoluble warmths
His hold however pensive
Sensed for greennesses
That blacken him

Leaves more earthen
And aloft
Thumb breezes
For a sport
More true than honest air can teach

Bark is no skin
So rightly ribbed
A vigil scarred, a trust
That quickens to a shield

Nor sun lodestone

That his own iron strive
Like no unarrowed thing
Above
To cleave leaf's origin

To greet arriving
What repose
As rooted and as raw
As any tree that is

The careless proof of seed and seed.

Death of the Poet

(*in mem.* B. Pasternak)

Wind riffling the hair the pages
And somewhere eyes on naked stalks—
Now the doors are standing slammed,
Small statues parry what music they can.

She pries in one or two small creases
But barely a trace along the shawl
Of the crude fidelity that bore her down—

There, in the lightning's breach, an instant—
There, within the thunder's rally—
No, he took the tally of his death along.

Late in the muddy rut of roadway
Bootprints tarry their dregs of rain,
The moon once more is made of smoke
Above a grave all knees and elbows.

IV

Statuary   SIX POEMS

1. Tags, or Stations

Tags, or stations, every bold
Approximate of everything, like leaves
The only pulp of what an autumn ought to be
Or landscape but the faltered posit,
Botched illation of a scenery;

Not this film and driven random
Purpose cannot bend, or take,
But what disarms the as-such of your aim
Pinned as were a street to the fake
Of direction only, only

The nisus of an argument, a hand
Fingered, nothing fingering, a word
The beating syllable of no word's voice
Or a footbeat no one walks toward
You, yourself the journey you rehearse.

2. All of This

All of this, the literal streets
Will never end, the steps, and pavement
Though you stop, or stop forever
Gripped to an immortal truth,
A word literal as one word only.

The flavor of this rain will lick you
Where you stand, where standing one
Or one emotion drowns your air:

You, where you are, eternal-eyed,
The apparition of what will, what iron
Archangel of its parable?

All this, the pavement, footsteps
And of rain, the long, the light of it
On metal, stone
                        —the throat's own violence
Deserts that cry, that silence
You, your posture, are perfected by.

3. Portrait

Ich bin ein Bild
Verlangt nicht dass ich rede.—Rilke

I spoke, my voice sounded,
And I heard: —as things that pause
Are brightened, cleared by angers—
Anger by desire wounded.

Far, far up the land
I found a shoreline, birds
Standing and no sea
Slapping it, nor wind

But arrested things
I could not hear;
Angers bent by angers,
Breath in the lungs stunned.

And my throat still instinct
With its pleasure
Started and was still,
The vein swollen, intact.

4. Sentinel

How shall we know him now
Who comprehends but one
Compassion any more? A window
Darkened always onto this
Same street, whatever passes;
Or a street cut off, and all
Its passage, at the frame of that
Same vantage—
                 an ignorance
That stands as though it were a center
Which nothing various
Could enter, or ever hope
To plagiarize.

5. L'Impasse des Deux Anges

Forget what route you travel here
To raise your outrage to the night—
Regard this now dead-ending square

Where two contrive one slant
Of combat locked, a boldness
Blind to the fury of its formal light.

Not all our sounded ways
Unculminate their single chord,
Not though we come tongue-humbled

Mumbling our meaning
Like deafened men, who trouble
Your arm, point where you cannot see

Nor seeing understand—
Regard these two, perpetual, firm,
Closed in struggle that cannot bend.

6. Covenant

Some other side of memory
And nothing still to think;
The soul consumed a heaviness
Of thirst it couldn't drink.

A stone-like hand regards
The cramp to lift its sword;
A vigilance falls down
Invidiously loud.

The year undoes its pride,
An innocent-seeming form;
A length of natural days
Equivalently looms.

Street and star appear
(If distance can be true);
Another sense to pledge,
A blank page given you.

Noon

And something not themselves, a thing
That lags, or overbends, a white
That waits in tightly knuckled things . . .

The buildings hold their height,
The air itself its care
For clarity, for outline, for the flight
Of birds
            —as though an emptiness
Could fall, or fill all space
With some forgottenness: that thing
Out of which nothing knows itself . . .

In every gesture of the face, the hand,
What loss or trust is mastering its ground?

Great Stroke of Noon that does not sound.

True Night

So it is midnight, and all
The angels of ordinary day gone,
The abiding absence between day and day
Come like true and only rain
Comes instant, eternal, again:

As though an air had opened without sound
In which all things are sanctified,
In which they are at prayer—
The drunken man in his stupor,
The madman's lucid shrinking circle;

As though all things shone perfectly,
Perfected in self-discrepancy:
The widow wedded to her grief,
The hangman haloed in remorse—
I should not rearrange a leaf,

No more than wish to lighten stones
Or still the sea where it still roars—
Here every grief requires its grief,
Here every longing thing is lit
Like darkness at an altar.

As long as truest night is long,
Let no discordant wing
Corrupt these sorrows into song.

Annus Mirabilis

Year of wonder, the virgin
Gleam and scent of oil
Of the olive, of the year
Cool and hushed and overall
Wine stops in the belly
Sheep puzzle the hillside
Begun looking, animals
Close toward the smell of angel

Hand petals breast, the virgin
Invents of womanly gesture
Hand disposed backward
Toward the hand of a child
Green and brown and stone
Connoiter, trees marry
Air, a bird alights
And is still, wings
Ruffle and are still, leaf
Holds color and the moon
Maintains phase and shadow

All things disassume
Their motions, flesh and
Memoryless moduli of sense
Winds die to edens of standing
Weather, nudities reestablish
As a sleeper wakes
As a trance resumes
A wrist holds thought
Of imminence, never.

Mythos

Shaping adventures where there are none
Back out of waiting, of return
The told assembles these lenient energies:
    A dwelling entered,
        A garment flung away.

Slack and image suffer to a sense
As limbs perfect a motive of their grip,
Possibility stained to a personal color:
    The sleepers dream,
        Dreamt by another's touch.

The plot will triumph where there is no plot,
The hero bedded in his stars
Show character at last candescent in its wake:
    Dawn rendered to a face,
        The night to a sounding dog.

Mythos (2)

Enter: each scrap of narrative
Defeated into weather. Sudden
As a light's importance, or a light
Shammed to the space intention seeks—
Committing stride against the walk
Of forward's amble, forward's ease
Frozen, finding the wind's lone tongue,
The hungering stopped ear: again, again, again.

The mind is slow, lets slip
This savage of its grasp. Mind
Knows itself diviner than it makes,
As pace is always disparate, inept
Against the light traversed things hold—:

All violences stayed and sudden light,
All pantomime and reason flayed
Between two edges:

                  life leaves its stories,
These this leaving take and live
The lease they claim, repeat the wind's
Unsunderable sweeps, the eager leaves
And the light again lingering in its place.

Visitations, Habitats

Visitations, habitats, hard and sundry
Currencies of sense which can stay, not
By reminiscence or redundancy, but as
Encounter strands a voice, or battle-
Scenes detain a color and a face

Outside the campaign's vigor or the war's
Result, such rigors of the mediate
Against all end: as here the arrow
Of your kiss uniquely blinds
Through the bright sorrows of all our days

Tell me that mind, the longest realism
Of now or will is powerless to speak
Direction of forgetfulness, or distance
Change; that the severest task
Will always be what truth we put

The twisting present to; that the man
Who holds you is the boy whom the sun
Burdened, whose loyalties grow dumb
Surviving dangers: as now to narrow
To your hair the fear no vow,

Not love's devoutest tyranny may fuse
Stray voices, no result of sorrows
Nor any message join those faces
Which resume each morning separately
To bleed unvaryingly the echo, the demand

Into every original or accumulated sun,
To borrow the most mated destinations
Of all bliss, the fear that broken
Splendor breaks us where we live, the life
We gather to our life we never own at all.

V

November Sunday Morning

And the light, a wakened heyday of air
Tuned low and clear and wide,
A radiance now that would emblaze
And veil the most golden horn
Or any entering of a sudden clearing
To a standing, astonished, revealed . . .

That the actual streets I loitered in
Lay lit like fields, or narrow channels
About to open to a burning river;
All brick and window vivid and calm
As though composed in a rigid water
No random traffic would dispel . . .

As now through the park, and across
The chill nailed colors of the roofs,
And on near trees stripped bare,
Corrected in the scant remaining leaf
To their severe essential elegance,
Light is the all-exacting good,

That dry, forever virile stream
That wipes each thing to what it is,
The whole, collage and stone, cleansed
To its proper pastoral . . .
                                I sit
And smoke, and linger out desire

And know if I closed my eyes I'd hear
Again what held me awake all night
Beside her breathing: a rain falling
It seemed into a distant stillness,
On broad low leaves beside a pond
And drop upon drop into black waters.

Stare at the Sea

Stare at the sea, the sea is blind.
The sea gives back your theme—
The sea that is not like, that cannot lack
A thing
            —you have heard this sea intoned
To every shock of chaos and of calm,
As though soul's torn two intellects
Would marry in that hollow heave
The harm they cannot fatalize, the thing
A stonier dumb charm would weave
Out of its own locked raging tides:
The sea holds nothing it can hide.

Teach the sea to sing, the soul
To drink its own imagining.

Swathes of March

Swathes of March, these days
And airs a high, thin shade of flint
—Important, personal, to go in your coat:
In the square a smoking chill, a light
That does not locate the sun;
And everything crossing, tree or life,
On its own, everything
Exactly inched toward an old exciting tooth
Of promise
    —Remembering your hair
    reverse the wind . . . Struck
That everything, everything
Writes into the clear middle of a page;
That never is there a place that is not
The miraculously turned margin of our lives.

Stills: From a 30th Summer

Shadow on a pavement,
    sunlit street,
smear of rainbow
    at the curb—
time is longer than the thought,
the playing out is slow.

Tangle of green grasses
    holds a page,
leaf-weakened light
    prints through—
what year of days has still to burn
before the stain wins through?

Poison of starlight
    on the sill,
love spilled over
    in the room—
life is everything it had to lose,
the losses broken into bloom.

Late Light

Gracious this candid pair of eyes—
I stir my cup, and let
the grain lie liquid.

Outside, the steam that rises
from tracks the gravel cannot hold
has entered a shade of the light.

Light I remember seeing
at a dry enduring stairwell,
an abandoned flight of stairs.

Day, Daylong

Day, daylong, how the soul goes staring
At its shoes, expanse that widens nakedly
To world
              where each is poised
Assassin, suicide, to wrest
Redemption of the other in its choice: yours
The helpless span narration cannot close.

Route nor spectacle will not go blind
Nor bind their broken conscience to a page:
Learn to be No-one in the voice of none,
Friend in that friendless element forever
Unbegun, a sea, a body, a remorse—

Take up this leaf: what do the dead,
The unborn defend? Your living syllable
Too mute, too loyal to its desuetude
To enter speech that does not speak
Consent, and claim, and failure to conclude.

Double Poem of Night and Snow

I

All, and more, still given, given you:
Each light that lames the avenue, the snow
That still can come to spaces veritably worn,
Long not your own. As though you slept. Or I
Sleep's sleeplessness to count without answer:
"Cold" and "street" and "star"—that where you wake
Or overtake me, nothing here resolve
To less than that these are.

II

Even in this light, these many points of light
That pierce the avenue, where weakly
A thin endeavor of snow sifts down: this thing
That goes and goes toward no root
                                    which rises—;
Even here whole candor fails, the cold
Is but your fever's brow: each lamp,
Pinpoint and aureole together flare.

Circumferences

Dawn under day, or dawning, lake, late edge,
Assumptive pure periphery where one thrust prominence
Now gives me back my eyes, my stride almost
A next abode, and source   O gathering, your smile
Is softer and more slow than the guileless surf
Drying forever at a farthest shore: I
Who have called you upright, destiny, or wall,
—How we exchange circumferences within
The one footfall that bruises us asunder.

Listening

I

Summer, Afternoon

This this will it always be, and why
To ever argue for: here walking
In its life, or sprawled, or loitering
Down shallow valleys of the lawn:
The trees that are there
The pigeon bobbing through
Its fallowgray ellipse of ground—
The comfort of this ground
Is physical: the sun
Goes through your shirt like liniment,

                The tilting
Child in fact now finding
Its first step, the blue balloon, the string
Of ducks drawn through the pond,
The twined twain, the air that hears
The day's gamegame, and where

Up through the cross-rack oak
Deep gladed lofts of leaf, green
Overtaking green and light and green
Array and hold
Their silent chord,
To where the vergemost
Quibble at clear nothing—there
Is not a purer ledge of opening; nothing
Here is not enough to be without
All need to ever argue for.

At Sunset

Grand gash of curtain light
Galled orange bleeding brown,
The sun will soon be licking
Where the towers tore him down.

And now this failing stain
Of the righteous lord of light
Torments the chimney pots, a smear
Of provocation runs under night,

As under your age, your innocence
Stiffens and gives away
Among the distracted mourners,
The galleried blank dismay.

Cancellations
1. Graffiti

The residual death of stones gave way
For the water to listen to utterly

Nothing here could go unreal
Though you cut as many cords at once

All paths were free (and did not lead)
To wrest in you their ruin, like any page
("All": ally: allay: alloy: allos:

Poynt said Carry, Lief said Glass
Shard said Semblant said Dance)

You had sometime divided a torrent
One wing of the drawbridge was fiction
That it knew how to span from your life

2. Hiatus: Between Waking and Waking

Long, far-green, . . . a fluttering wing—
(Above the weight, beneath my ear your eyelid seemed—)
When heavily I stepped again, my field,
Had it been golden-flooded?—Oh,
The far low hills now darkening . . .

Nightfall

The evening slips another rung—
Then one more flaring coal
Breaks down the fading inks

Whose colors drown (among the roofs),
The tide fills one last crevice out.

The rock of dark divides its noon
With trees alive as wolves
As past the park, all stranded light wins through.

II

Listening FOUR POEMS

1. Morning, Arraignment with Image

That wave that high turning that
Once disresembled that
Once disremembered a future—
Now its wake broad conscripting suffices
And leaves a roomful of years unmolested . . .
Except for this short pre-morning of truck sounds,
This barrack of seasons no longer embodied;

You thought to have proffered an image of justice
But the fall of that wave now
But the scroll of that wave now
Is heartbreak terror and boldness knowing
That justice that hates you
Your eyes its own eyes and our shame.

2. The Listening Beasts, the Creatures

They had not heard of song; but some strange
Superfluity of what was most themselves
Seemed newly to be recognizing them:
Why was this overing in the man so sad?

Uneasy, something wonted strove to roar
But the ravelling throat lay listening
To the last imprisoning notes, that lowly vouched
His own, that then could tell the faltering spell
Binding fingers at the lyre, the eyes that gazed
At nothing, the now sounding body, stone.

3. Then Leda

True you must take her by surprise
Among the thrice-insistent reeds
You had bested thought, you had worsted thought
   Of cutting binding blowing;

By surprise as though it were herself
About to lead you, hold you to the part
Where you are let forget, where you are let beget
   Yourself the reeds the waters flowing:

Where then the head docile and hard
Against her tendered breast seems cruel
If not lordly and the arms breakingly
Embracing all their lost disdain
Seem wings that vaunt themselves
   To merely gain the ground;

Where then as she breathes you hear again
The alien triumphant inhumanly audible sound.

4. False Night, or Another

Night, this must be your false voice
I hear, or else your last; for you know as I
That the one who lingers at this ramp
Is not the one you would harass
Who is surely gone, and without eyes, down
As to the root of a black azure, or channel
That refuses up its course
Back to the face that knows you,

That to your mist and imprecation
Turns, as the death-flower turns
As do faces that unsleep your story
And all spaces, come to this,
Where no-one, not un-privileged,
Listens where still your innocent design
Assails what is not summoned in its name.

Wet Pavement

Spring. Night. Rain. And
The street gives back a starry vine,
Young old incontrovertible grape—
The seasoned arteries of sense
May taste unspeculative wine.

Second Marriage Song

(for Jane and Stanley)

What best than this day's morning's
Gray for all of autumn's tracings near
To unseen shining to come clear

As bittersweet's gay spiralling
Among black honey-locust branch
Above fields longer far than snow

And smoke, bright trellising in air—
This sprig of wandering's waking clear
As dreaming, as forever near.

Thanksgiving Day, 1987
North Bennington, Vermont

The Unpublished Poems

When Alvin Feinman died in 2008, he left behind a small cache of documents, about 200 manuscript pages. Deborah Dorfman, Alvin's widow, had been transcribing and editing this manuscript for several years by the time I contacted her in the summer of 2014. I studied with Alvin during the mid-1980s at Bennington College and had always wondered if he had written more poetry than what had been published during his lifetime. Talking to Deborah, I discovered that indeed he had. The manuscript contained dozens of poetic fragments and 48 unpublished poems in various stages of completion, 39 of which are published here. Deborah and I decided to put together a complete edition of Alvin's poetry—the text of the 1990 edition of *Poems* plus the unpublished work we deemed in finished form.

Early on in the process, I asked Deborah what Alvin would have thought of what we were doing. After all, he chose not to publish these poems while he was alive. Why should we?

Deborah felt strongly, as I do, that Alvin's work deserves a much wider audience than it has so far achieved. His poems have remained largely unknown in part because he published so little. We also agreed that the unpublished poems are as fully realized and astonishing as those he did choose to publish. Together with *Poems*, the work appearing here for the first time establishes Alvin as one of the great American poets of the twentieth century, alongside Hart Crane and Wallace Stevens, with whom his poetry and poetics have so much in common.

There is also evidence that Alvin himself would not have objected to the publication of these poems, all of which were written in the mid- to late 1950s, at the same time as the work in *Preambles and Other Poems*. An early table of contents for *Preambles*, found among the manuscript pages, features many of the unpublished poems, indicating that Alvin considered including them. In his notes for a reading he gave at Bennington, probably in the spring of 1970, Alvin listed several unpublished poems as part of the sequence he wished to read. And, with one exception—"Second Marriage Song," written in 1987—the poems Alvin added to *Preambles* for the publication of *Poems* in 1990 came from this same collection of unpublished work, including "This Tree," the only poem that can be precisely dated: October 10, 1956.

Deborah had almost finished editing the unpublished poems (we decided not to publish any of the fragments) by the time she died in the summer of 2015. Vivian Heller, a colleague and former student of Alvin's at Bennington College, and I completed that work.

—James Geary

I

The Way to Remember Her

Take only this, the hand, the flower
In her hand, imagine, do not look,
Her eyes, her lips, call that delight—
    And burn the name of it.

Dispel the reasons from your lips
And what it comes to, lips, and eyes,
The held flower always in the end—
    And burn the name of it.

And tear from what your voice intends
The word it tells you or the thought
Reminds, beginning, end, again—
    And burn the name of it.

    —Or burn that hand, the lips,
The eyes, the flower, all, all save
The knowledge, the desire that kills
And leaves the burning name of it.

For Lucina

Neither beginning, nor ending
Neither first, nor final fire
Nor the savored salt of indecision . . .

For the sun hangs
      like a leaden crust
          weary of color
cold and skeletal as desire in an idiot's palm.

Neither speech, nor vision . . .

For the day crumbles
      into ciphers
words litter the streets like dirty snow

And where you look
      the children
start and hobble like achondroplasts.

But the time of silence joined
The time of wedded darknesses.

Letter to Jane

I took your hand, the wind blew
dust and bits of paper, you narrowed
your eyes, smiling, your lips drawn,
parted, your face turned
sideward, strangers passing
and the cars, the busses and their
noise, and the heels on the street
and the voices, and I
letting your fingers slip away and
one or both of us said goodbye

And all the way that night riding
I saw the twilight sinking,
our eyes wet, hardly speaking,
a warm breeze later through the window,
and the wonder
of loveliness passed upon us.

For Enid and Jerry

Slowly on the evening air
this dance of summer stillness
along the lithe ailanthus leaves.

Through the window above my bed,
I watch the slender leaves, the fronds
that graze the brown brick wall and rain-
gutters long since turned to rust.

On the bed hand in hand my friends are lying
and in my heart their love dances slowly
as ailanthus leaves that play the air
and greenly brush the weathered wall.

Soliloquy of the Lover out of Season

Could I have owned in that midtime
With crossed winds driving toward the hilt,
My arm half risen and fingers
Seeking the actual fist, eastward
The winds and westward crossing, the virtual
Stature a mirror mocking my driven
Posture, the crossing winds at my source's center
Like silent wolves the oldest men remember
Tail-down in the sparse timber, my animal
Exile tracking the natural scent
Through snow half worn, half blanketing
The green and somber outrage of birth,
Of dying, of mixed winds at the seasons' crossing,
Could I have known my own love's color

Have mocked my winter of unvouched issue
Nor bled of the white beginning
To ride love's roused and ventured pennants
Mindless as tooth and tongue could tell
The promise they commit, nor riddle heark
From hindsight weather that proud
I might bear you an anchored thing
Confirmed of rock and the sun's blessed tether,
Deaf-held to that midtime questioning,
That flaunt and jostle of whichway winds
Aloud with anonymous wisdom's curse and the evil
Of old man's augurings, lest gift be a loosed
And jetsam thing, but driftage seized
Where winds beguile and love be but a foundering,

Have dared divide a quartered man
To bride him whole by love's despotic color?

The Reading

Where he stands, knee-levered, bird-like
As the boy is man-like that he bears,
Disarmed and stilting, so the towsled talk
Disdains presumption or an air
Applause dissimulates—
Before us now the necessary guise,
Behind the lean gratuities
Umbilical still with held surprise—

Of winds whipping a dark pocked coast,
A headland slouched toward lumbering tides
Where gulls crack out their bounty on rock
Dive down and tear the bruised insides
Difficult bounty the fisher prides

As wall, and window, strict,
Ungenerous hour, the pledgeless bird
Grip-shifting on its branch, constrict
Their closure to a world—wall, window,
Podium—that bird's essential
Mercenary stare
Remakes his word the token of its lust—
Can he demand that he restore
What his all self-centered trust transacts to litany—

Of loss, of forfeiture the tethered rush,
The drummed swell singled to a cry
As of a bird, a lonely caller, raker
Of the tide's broad monied after-slush

Thinned to original girlhood now
The rag-end of her garment trails
Along the aisle, her eyes
Hinged back to idle aftermaths her hands—
Whose cane crashes
O Lady, Why does no one smile—

Where back the dune and windward rise
Assemble toward the fabled house;
The childhood harvest seasoned in the shed,
High windows shuttered, knockings of the god

Retrieve your wand, unstricken bird
It is the body of his own bled mind
His word, your vacant gaze, exhumes,
A coin you cannot use
Nor any brother in the mutual womb.

Sunset with Male Figure

I could believe it is the last red wash of light
is sinking, drying, down and fading
and the slow, the final turning
of some wide and brilliant, ancient whirling
stilled to this sweet, this blood-dim dying.

I could believe it is a total ending,
a world-waning, I could believe it is <u>too-late</u>
<u>too-late</u> the distant bird is singing
trapped out in the closing suck
of a summer evening,
<u>too-late</u> and oh, <u>too-late</u>, but the sweet
and silent gather of all single, lonely wasting,

but to meet
your eyes' proud, final flaring, greet
as we turned, each toward his releasing,
the weakness, splendor of the man you are.

[untitled]

Your eyes, quick then with the ring of distances
are onyx, twin hieroglyphs
graven in some season of belief, dark now to the touch.

Your eyes fierce then in augury,
enprismed in their pillared sight, enoracled,
I clasped the kiss of savage possibility,
enjoined the gyrant heart's futuric thrust—
High realms of destined vision crumble under bone,
wild silences inflect your delphic dust.

And flames that sauntered then
along the leaping banners of your glance
Many told and dazzled blood up-wizarded—
to drown the bartered blaze, dispel
and disensinew all but the etched inconsequence
that burns to blackness in the cryptic stone.

The seasons whiten into flameless days,
Spent blood turns fossil in the flesh,
Your dark and amulet eyes yet once again inherit me.

[untitled]

Until you have crossed the desert and faced that fire
Love is an evil, a shaking of the hand,
A sick pain draining courage from the heart.—Sidney Keyes

It is a young man's admonition
a young man's pride, foreknowing
It is the wind's first curse among the saplings.

Let the red sun stand, such shammed
Blood as gathered Eden's gloom within
The world's first darkness whelms
As then
                    As then
It is the iron and shattered fact
Will not lie still among the foresworn
Seeds: As then time will take but in hand,
The body find its need—
Our knowledge will prove useless

[untitled]

Vivid beauty shot the sprawling tides
Your eyes infixed their paling
        into memory
Though the clouds' compatibilities
Implied no breach—no want of cloudly
        continuities

In the evening of the tides, the choice again
    was yours
Our bodied closure hot upon the sand
The sea-swell brandishing its moon
Your arms divided from your arms

That blue and arching swathe of stars
Could chill the contest of our thighs
Or blind grip blood that moon

There are inveterate pure passages and
    impure interdictions:
Eyes that follow longingly their
    very vision
To reclaim, to gather ends

      Such ache for stars
must mark a fallacy of being, we
are wounded
leaping after tides.

A Farewell to the Grammarian of the Heart

You stood beside me at the edge of land
Where waves surrender to the ear
Fingering saltless froth
And told the gull's great arc
An outer paradigm

As where she lay upon the sands
You measured moonlight flung
Abroad the sea's warped screen
Whitely as a shark's lust numbs
Amid stranded shells.

Inherit then my agile ghost
The mirror and the mirror-eye
Against what known
Uncharted isthmus we had wrung
Of splendid penury

My foolish hands had lief unlearn
By fabled blindings of her flesh
What thunders flare
The shoulders of the waves, what moons
Swing close and hot.

In Praise of Space and Time

1.

Well I understand your love of distances.
One dreads the most the superable:
imagine the moon indoors!

What should become of us if not for space?
To be always where one is—
think of Orestes unpursued,

But closeted among those crones his "fate,"
his rootedness had spawned
in the rank ancestral ground . . .

God's brain alone, His heaven is dimensionless.
Shall I deny the roundness of your thigh,
or the geometry of grace?

2.

Mark how the moment shuttles in the square.
Red, now green, now red again—
What could Plato know of constancy?

Time's very blood expends, redeems itself; here
there is no need for hope—eternity!
and one dares breathe.

Let eschatologists cry, "Stop, enough!"
Let there be nothing new, when leaving:
I'll spin the wheel again.

Salvation, rest—the fixed idea of jugglers
driven to a point of view . . . There,
do not hold me quite so close.

II

Intruder

It comes to illustrate, no more.
A pretext, nothing
                    more: to stone
a lending to itself
the need of itself
                    the dog
intruding to the street, alone,
to the street's impressionable weather;
stranding the swiftly human
a word is surer than;
                        dogging a world
not all this just-so light
can trust, solidify. But here
unreasoned, pure, exemplum
                            this:
a thing stricken in a pebbled light.

Lament for the Coming of Spring

Dumb as the continuity of rock
light forsythia rags the fevered air:
spasms of jaundiced joy.
Ivy rattles on the wall.

Petals quicken to enwomb
the scabrous passion of the bee,
ache as Leda in the shuddering reeds
to clasp this hairy paraclete.

While strident-eyed, the squirrel
scatters noon with skinny hands:
deaf dionysian acolyte,
tropistic maggots pince his brain.

Alas, what dark, what terrible,
what holy winter dying holds
against this helic hate?

Backyard, Hoboken, Summer

The sun beating on his brain
And a cat slouching on the woodpile
And flies nauseous with heat

He holds three eternal parameters
The habit of his eye repeats
The shapes he reifies

Let the silence silence its own ache

There is nothing but the plenum of a small red brain

The flies fall suppurant among the sticks
The cat prepares for life

As though the moveable could move
Even the impossible recedes

As though within the clot of brain
Were space or sun to make a world

Evening in the Gentile Town

Here along these quiet streets
trees receive the heavy light
of afternoon, sealing themselves
in mute communion with high erratic houses

And air, a lavender absence
of motion, temperature and pulse
where distance settles like an unplied
venture tuned to imaginable looming things . . .

You too are part of an uncharted
credulence that wells: it is as though
these things were meant to be, it is
as though you were the man who walks here weightlessly;

As though the hand that gloves your own
had tricked this narrow lapse of lust
that finds your fallow angers drowned,
distracted, interdict within a widened moment's chastity

Where a voiceless man intones:
O Lion of the World where stalks your threat?
O Heart where is your thorn? Where,
O Son of Man, the flare, the lightning in your streets?

The autumned streets are still,
even as the trees stand stripped
uncertainties are spent, inert
and grave where noons and terrored nights succumb,

Where faiths and furies and betrayals sink.
No spirit dawdles doomfully within this brink.

The Islander

Each day he paced the silver edges of the sea
an islander caged in its silver ribbings
brandishing whatever ease or violence
its echoes lend
and the steel enormity of an orbless eye

slaking the lava fury of the sun
with jewel craft
dispelling what it dare not dominate
to master its own voluptuous jaws
even as islanders are drowned
by what they cannot comprehend.

He read lust's glint and mirrored analogue
aslant the vast contraction of an iron pride's
cold fluid metal mastery
the spendthrift treasury of island reefs
of shoals it slaughters to caress
as chain all sinews of the windy air
within one blue inviolable will
even as islanders confound
land-locked resolve in shifting sand.

"Wisdom is tidal, is success
it is your white death-splendid oneliness
the self-delivered blaze that suckles you
your walled sufficiency
whose broad mercuric amplitudes
roll mockeries of gender at my feet."

Caged in the silver ebbings of the shore
the islander turns: loud gulls slow-circling
and their mates
who feed where the tides withdraw.

Matinal

White maned morning vaults the spume,
The trumpet drum of wave on rock;
Blasting the jeweled light apart
Each gothic aerial shock
Rides warrior wind like a helmet plume
As chariot riot drinks the heart,

The weathered eye and flesh of me
Out-voiced, out-fabled, rung:
Some brine archaic Mastery roars
Clarion laughter flung
Tideward astride the glistening knee
Of cliffed and echoing shores

Where wild god-bridled terrors joy
My thundered pulse; not I,
Some lashed stone presence wakes
To wield, to quicken, buoy
This thrill galvanic gusto sky-
Ward where sun-slashed heavens break,

To chant the reins of spirit skilled
To bone, as is thy sling
Of brilliance turmoil bound,
Thy mounted salvos drilled
Past dare of conjuring
The paean of tempest deafness drowned:

Wave shattering wave past sense,
Past power commute the breath,
O epic tempo of no birth or death
Blastbind the blood thy reverence.

III

Socratic Adieu

For all the belly's backward reason
It seemed I asked the season death,
Thinking no rot thereby to gut's
Gay tooth, but a withered branch of brain
Releasing poisoned fruit:
No matter.
The sun-drunk birds had surely left me,
Dropping upward one by one,
I taking leave of the loan of my eyes
And the troubled filling of abstract man
Equally flayed of whichever failure.

.

Neither/Nor

No more the moment's core;
I have chosen nothing
As a hawk dares

To bleed an essence
In one plunge
Not to learn;

Nothing, as a leaf turns
Sunward, surer than
The gull's cold wing

Or anguish of the annelid:
White will of distances
Or the marrow's mesh.

I have chosen not again
To choose to pierce
The perfect center

Of each perfect rose, but hold
One wisest pain
Till telic heat

Refuse the sunlight
and the final passion
Of my year's return.

Song

Water buds in the water-tap
Words bubble up within the mind
The highways curve across the map
The light crawls down the blind

A diamond splinters in the sink
The nouns digest their verb
Collision closes like the rose
Two moons are kissing at the curb.

Song for Evening

The traveler in me is weary, who walks
    the bridges of evening that span
no visible shores, toward the darkness
    which beckons and forewarns.

My wanderer wends toward darkness
    where the moonlit music of flutes
weaves a silver and velvet doublet
    to shroud his widowed heart.

Weary though he be, and his heart grown
    single with grief, I fear
he will not rest; the bridge thrusts
    endlessly onward, the music lures.

Though he press onward, I shall abide,
    let weather who will, or fall.
I have turned my heart toward silence
    that binds and chastens like mail.

Postlude for the Metaphysician

Wild rider of the rarest tides, you
Who savored the husks of innocence
Grown gorgeous for the feel of your hand,
Who scored the Devourer's blackest belly
Under an arched and beating wing;

Marking as it were
The trip-
A-trip of counters on a cracked roulette,
The nacre telos of Mind's
Warped uterine Nothing.
And the weal of the fortunate face:
No breath clouds *le miroir du monde*,
We are safe on every side, ringed
By grave gratuities.

Now the rinds of your eyes wax ripe
Necessities roll like squandered beads
Not to be gathered, not to be eaten, these
Pips of fallen fruit that split the glass
Like light
                    Where you descend
Now face to face down familiar ways
Toward the total kingdom, treading
Your wagers underfoot, to greet
The juggler of fabulous eggs
Who yet foretells
The issue of credible fecundations:

Life is division of distances,
Small potencies the Jamesian triggers;
The wanton tracings of a skinny demiurge.

[untitled]

The rain drives darkly down
the grim ungainly roofs and gutters
of the town; the blackness whelms to drown
our clouded windows, and the shutters
mute no light or sound, but where
the tower bells assault the smoking air

blasting with time the rotted
soldier in the square.

Speak now in high hieratic tones
of dissolution and the curse of time
the gutted towers and crumbled bones
of seer and satrap and the gentle mime
invoke our manacled ancestral fright
that haunts the raven-bellied aisles of night.

Epilogue: Zone and Invocation

Roof and region of unbecome
Garland of distances, cloud-cameo'd
Forehead for now, Air
outside a hospital, Courtyard
of the street's imprisoned crops
Element, Survivor in me, Cushion
of stars, Bird-point, Zone
through which the moon lengthens, Wake
of memories like futures, Abyss
trustworthy as pockets, Communard
Imperator
          —give me
to confound nothing in your auspices.

The Innocents

To forego the prodigy of verse
That each speaking thing
Might utter itself only,
Its hapless uncompounded sense.

That each air's wand
In the element of its happening
Unawaitedly cover
And draw unmournably off:

That naming was the terrible power
Gathering the last
Against its time,
The Midas miracle.

Till the entrusted ones,
The obliterators,
Absolved their sentence also—
The salt of itself singing.

[untitled]

Amber as a lucency of earth.

Let amber be blue's pagelessness hungrier over
grasses, a proffering of great stone fingers to
conjoin the regions of sun and wasp.

Nor without fascination abandoned in the lark's
shadow; that where the fountain falls in its own
ear, it will seem the poem of muter entrance . . .

Amber, the poem behind the name of blue.

[untitled]

Snow. Tree tranced. O silent
It would be outside. Dark it would be
And caged in moonlight. Half afraid
To go, and needing to, to know, not
Knowing what to know, to stand
And need the words, and need to not
Need words for white and cold, and far
And lone, and lovely sighing dark
Like nothing, like a leg,
A cheek pleased in the cold,
A furred eye flaking into light.

Preamble for a Stone Age

Because the ways of faith as of despair
have been rehearsed and are well-known,
charted in chastity or lust, and noisily
dispensed or cherished secretly; because
recovery and murder are one,

Because the wise or innocent holds his tongue
as well for others' sake as for his own;
because wisdom crumbles in formula and innocence
when plied—deeper therefore than will or pride,
imponderably hewn as found, as though

In rock ineffable; inviolate, all-silencing the sanctifying word is bound.

What as of rock will be told or bartered,
will be flourished, echoed, coined, in incorruptible
copy charted? What as of rock will stone
the sense past vision, evasion, prescience?
What of the dense pre-ambience of rock,
pre-movable, pre-posited will ground
or hold or bind this turning and this
vacancy?

Lo, lithic realisms wall the air, contain
the habitations we expend, Lo, gravities dark
as onyx shall bind our leavings to ourselves.

Stanzas for W. B. Yeats

To hold in a single thought reality and justice.—W. B. Yeats

1.

The shelf is crowded, overflowed,
A yellow heap upon the floor.

The guardian out, or gone to sleep,
A puzzled wind goes from the door.

The wheel slips over, stutters, chokes,
The horses fled, the cart spilt on its side.

The lovers lift one burning face,
The moon cracks like a glass.

Here stands a pack of trees and here
A chimney breaks the evening's back.

The young tear up their names into the stream,
Eternity will not inherit more.

2.

How shall I portion history or
Take the senseless human task to heart?—
Many take down a golden mask
And weep, and how the tears
Seem golden on their cheek.

As though below that agony of gold
Were something dumber and without a name,
A thing that if it wished to speak
Would teach a way to tell
What gold may not exchange,

Where all are bound to ignorance
And death if death is that living thing
That cracks within the bell of speech
Or moans and tinkles
When winds thresh the rubbish heap.

IV

Song of the Dusting Woman in the Library

What is it holds the scholar to his desk
These nameless days, and through the long
Uncounted years? Is it the use of tears
He works to understand? Is it the song
He seeks that has not yet been sung?

And will he sing then when the tome
Is shut, the last word's echo in his brain?
And will he weep then when the last
Idea is hung, when he has wrung
The name, the origin, the issue of each pain?

Natura Naturans

Nor hope nor memory nor plan
how, knowing not to know,
to hold, beyond these triple prongs of pain

the soaring bird, entrust
through fathomed distances,
bloodborne, the sun's unerring wing, adjust

the gesture to the root,
mold silence within sound
and, womb-blue day, each prescience refute,

the mocked brain consecrates
your art—though eyes go blind
within this woman-will your blaze creates

as scandent shadows cleave
the evening wall to probe
cold stone, in vain to re-enact, believe

the windless thrust, the breath,
the turning of the leaf:
as blood forgets, the brain revives to death.

An Heretic to Heretics

Let be, forget the words we made
And rolled in celebration on our tongues
Lest it be deemed thus much a staying;
—The unbetraying ass sports heritage,
Dark donkeydoms inflect his braying—

Lest diction, surrogate—that faith
To shadow forth the old good grace
Round and total, gainsaying;
Told ghosts corrode the apostate pledge
Whose tropes are relic of our praying.

Forget. If not the flesh of praise
The word is a vain, self-mocking thing
However lyric, sweet the naying;
Let silence be, the parent dead,
A bloodless moon, cold tides obeying.

A Motive for the Fallacy of Imitative Form

Perfectness more perfectly somehow cheats,
leaves you suddenly facing paper.
Not the monotone irreal of flawlessness
—that you transact in another coin,
barter to your toy and civil need.

But the excellent, the relevantly good
precisely lets you down, the taste already
member through your belly and alongside
knowing it does no personal good.
Nor is it a question of warts on the toad,

of stippled fish and all ornate
roughage. I mean the necessary, driven
failure, breaks and losses, the bare ineptness
of loose-ended venture, and the awkward
dogged original gangle where the seed

falls tentative, impatient, unimproved,
adamant of very craft, convention. Dire
or innocent, in any case strung
where there isn't time, where the after-thought
is the act's betrayal. Anti-

perfect if you will. Life is. Besides,
perfection, for all is said, insists
its strategies, will lastly discomplete itself
in the honed closure of its own intention,
will lose you outside, past

the stoppage, shift, the grip, the severance
that masters it. Not as an apple ripening,
natively being the fruit of its own
unreasoning. But the will say to style
eventuate, the upshot parried, art is,

of what entered at first a challenging not
alone to name, not only in arrest to dominate.

Fragment for the Necessary Angel

If needing a more unculminated world
Or harsher in every shape the tentative,
The pang and tentative of action's stealth,
That vision not be crux of vision's competence
As memory is rose, rose sovereign of sight
All dereliction ransomed in the bud,
The accurate passion of your passioned art

Is not arraigned for little differences,
Honoring the debt one paid to tame the hush
And stutter of the eye's unwieldy perpetual design,
The vibrant and the black of things unreconciled
Sighted sufficient at last to sight, to music
The perfect surgeon of its melody, there always sounding
The dark luminous nerve of necessary reverence.

The True Spain

Consonance of hill and shoulder
And beyond the graven valley.

And the sun a low sepulchral monarch
Red as habit slaughtered
In mysterious inclusions:
An end to paraphrase, the decimal encounter.

Above the inveterate leaf, the pale cone of the locust;
Within, the thigh-bound lilt of thirst—

Then the guitar, the blood-stemmed voice no older.

Remorse is full unknowable heart—
The gulf become desire is its song.

Moon

You, too, are a machine
And the clean tirade
Of your yellow fevers
Glistens all ways through the history of things.

      Along the land
The steel slopes that saddle you
And the lean trees ribbed to your rhythms;
Cool, your burnings buzz the wilds,
And the hard crops lathed to your phases.

Moon-engine, wheel, breast, belly, knob
Oiler of the churn of the ground's going,
Dimpler of its kiss and every fruit
Slickens the hug of the land's leaning.

City is your rubbed and hummed machine
Alive to the clock of your intricate balances,
And the silver shape of every season
Machined to available pities

Tower and stack to tap your turnings,
Tune the streets to your tooled design.

Man and boy, the women
In gold and yellow windings, gold
As the moon's mechanical fevers
Listen in the city, machined rejoicers:

Click me, says the moon,
In your blood's bright ribbon,

Hum me, says the moon,
In your will's white rhythms

Mine me, says the moon,
In the round machine of your body,
I am the true machine of your story.

War Dance of the Apocalyptic Pagan

Apple my mouth lord, game the waste,
Blood will green the blazing morrow,
Let the monied die be cast:
Let thirsted talons jag the sparrow,
Virgin mothers wick their lust;
The trigger wind will teach my arrow,
Bellies munch the bodied host.

Fuel my whoop lord, gaud the grass,
Let spruce wolf-tooth the gully's sliver,
Venom sweet the sassafras:
Mantic tides will whip the river,
Fat priapic bison stomp;
The juggler sun will luck my quiver,
Spank the canyon's torpid rump.

Bride my boast lord, flesh the dust,
The thigh's string will not waver,
Let thy jumping thunder blast:
Let hunger gird the bled boy saver,
Beggars trump the mourner till;
As word is foil and ghost no giver,
Let warriors ride thy target will.

Stone Anatomies

We must be lost in stone
>in water
>into stone
>be quenched
>in fire, dissolved and stoned
>in fire

We must be numbed
>in stone
>to wood, in wood's
>stone jelly boned
>be whet
>in air, in air's fierce
>drownings fired

Our beauties must be charred in wood
>through stone, through cutting water
>leafed

We must descend through stone's
>soft foot, through sear and atom honed
>of nothing, out of nothing stained
>to stone

Our hands must sprout
>from starfish stone, from rain
>our fingers and from rain
>and stone's dissolve of air
>our breathing
>and blood's breathing
>beat to hair

From leaf and water seal
>to wood
>in bone, in bone's
>red leafing
>fire
>the nostril into brain

The eye must beat
    in lizard light, in stone
    into the head's webbed bone

That stone enough be loss to start the lung.